Balance From Within: Autoimmunity, Stress, and the Path to Resilience

By: Speaking Freedom Books

Concept By: Kaci (Winslow) Myers

ISBN: 978-1-944901-47-9

Copyright © 2025 by Speaking Freedom LLC
All rights reserved.
No portion of this book may be reproduced without written permission from the publisher or author, except as permitted by U.S. copyright law.

Book Cover by: Kaci Winslow

Publisher Website: speakingfreedom.org

Other Website Information:
SpeakingfreedomTV.org, edu-freedom.org

Publisher Address: 75 Washington St. #1177, Fairburn, GA 30213

Dedication

This book is dedicated to **Ineka Adams**, my childhood friend, whose strength and battle with lupus continues to inspire resilience and compassion.

It is also dedicated to all those living with autoimmune conditions, as well as to the caregivers, families, and loved ones who support them.

May these pages bring understanding, encouragement, and a reminder that healing is possible, even when the path feels uncertain.

Introduction

Living with autoimmunity is rarely straightforward. For many, it begins quietly with unexplained fatigue, scattered joint pain, mood swings, brain fog, and stomach upset. Symptoms that might be dismissed as "normal stress" or "getting older" can gradually take root, leaving people searching for answers that never seem to arrive. By the time a clear diagnosis is given, months or even years may have passed. For some, the search for clarity never ends.

This book was written to address the frustration with **understanding, offer compassion, and provide tools for resilience**. It does not offer a miracle cure. Instead, it offers a framework to help you understand what's happening inside your body, how stress and lifestyle influence your immune system, and what steps can bring balance back into reach.

Why This Book Matters

Autoimmune conditions affect more than **50 million people in the United States alone** and millions more worldwide. They strike across age, gender, and cultural background. They do not discriminate, yet they disproportionately affect women, particularly during times of hormonal change. They intersect with trauma, emotional stress, financial strain, and reproductive health. And still, they remain misunderstood.

Understanding autoimmunity means looking beyond a single lab result. It means recognizing patterns, exploring the relationship between emotions and physiology, and accepting that healing is layered, gradual, and deeply personal. That is the purpose of this book: to empower you to see the bigger picture of your health while offering practical steps for change.

Who This Book Is For

- **Those newly diagnosed**, looking for clarity in a sea of medical jargon.

- **Those still searching for answers**, who feel dismissed or unheard.
- **Caregivers and loved ones** who want to understand what their friend or family member is experiencing.
- **People managing PTSD or chronic stress**, who may not realize how profoundly the nervous system shapes immunity.
- **Practitioners and students** who want to understand autoimmunity in a whole-person context.

Each chapter explores each layer of the autoimmune puzzle:

Chapter 1 - Understanding Autoimmunity: What autoimmunity is, why diagnosis can be complex, and how inflammation works in the body.

Chapter 2 - Stress and Emotions: The biology of being overwhelmed, how stress hormones and emotions fuel immune imbalance.

Chapter 3 - Trauma, Triggers, and the Body: How

unresolved experiences can imprint on the nervous and immune systems.

Chapter 4 - Reproductive Health and Hidden Diagnoses: Endometriosis, cysts, hormone shifts, and how they complicate autoimmune care.

Chapter 5 - Genetics, Environment & Early Development: Family patterns, environmental inputs, and early-life influences.

Chapter 6 - Conception, Surrogacy & Immune Beginnings: How the health of egg, sperm, pregnancy, and the womb environment lays the first roots of immunity.

Chapter 7 - Blood Type Health & Genetics: Blood type tendencies, ancestry, epigenetics, and what they (do and don't) mean.

Chapter 8 - Supportive Practices & Reframing Stress: Tools to regulate the nervous system and reframe setbacks without toxic positivity.

Chapter 9 - Financial Insecurity & Health: How money stress drives flares, blocks access to care, and what resources can help.

Chapter 10 - Lifestyle Integrations: Bringing nutrition, movement, stress relief, and community into daily life in sustainable ways.

Appendix - Tools & Resources: Trackers, journaling prompts, visit prep, flare-day plans, financial scripts, and quick references you can use immediately.

What This Book Is Not

This book is not a replacement for medical treatment. It does not promise a cure or suggest that lifestyle changes alone are enough. Instead, it provides support you can use alongside your medical team, empowering you to participate actively in your care and recovery.

A Note of Reassurance

You are not alone. Living with autoimmunity can feel isolating, but millions walk this path. By weaving together science, lived experience, and practical tools, this book gives you more than knowledge: that it gives you hope, perspective, and resilience. Healing is not a straight line, but balance is possible step by step, layer by layer, from within.

Chapter 1

Understanding Autoimmunity

Autoimmunity can feel like a betrayal, as if your body has turned against you. In reality, it is a case of mistaken identity. The immune system, which separates typically "self" from "not-self," begins to misfire. Instead of just fighting viruses, bacteria, or damaged cells, it sometimes mistakes healthy tissue for an enemy. The result is a constant internal battle that you never signed up for.

This mistaken attack leads to **inflammation,** swelling, pain, and damage that can affect almost any part of the body. In one person, it might show up as painful, swollen joints; in another, as digestive problems; and in another, as rashes or crushing fatigue. No two journeys are the same, which is why autoimmune diseases often feel so isolating.

The Diagnosis Maze

One of the hardest parts of living with autoimmunity is the **diagnosis journey**. Symptoms often **mimic other conditions**:

- Fatigue that looks like depression or burnout.
- Digestive upset that resembles food intolerance.
- Brain fog that could be mistaken for stress or anxiety.
- Joint pain that gets dismissed as "just aging."

Because of this overlap, many people spend **years searching for answers**. They may hear, *"your labs look normal,"* or *"it's probably stress,"* more times than they can count. That uncertainty can feel maddening, and it adds emotional strain on top of physical symptoms.

If you've ever been told "it's all in your head," this book is here to tell you **it's not.** What you are experiencing is real, and you are not alone.

The Spectrum of Autoimmune Conditions

Researchers have identified **over 80 autoimmune conditions**, ranging from the well-known (such as lupus, rheumatoid arthritis, and multiple sclerosis) to the quieter ones that often slip under the radar (such as Hashimoto's thyroiditis or celiac disease).

Each condition wears a different face:

- **Lupus** may present as joint pain, rashes, or kidney problems.
- **Multiple sclerosis** affects the nervous system, causing weakness or numbness.
- **Hashimoto's thyroiditis** attacks the thyroid, usually leading to underactive thyroid (hypothyroidism).
- **Graves' disease** also targets the thyroid, but in the opposite way, driving it into overactivity (hyperthyroidism).
- **Celiac disease** creates digestive chaos in response to gluten.

Different names, different symptoms, but the same root problem: an immune system that has lost tolerance for its own body.

Why Does It Happen?

Think of your immune system like a smoke alarm. Typically, it goes off when there's a real fire. In autoimmunity, the alarm becomes overly sensitive, going off when you burn toast, light a candle, or sometimes for no clear or apparent reason at all.

Why does this happen? There's no single cause. Instead, think of it like a scale that tips when too much weight is added:

- **Genetics** loads the scale with predisposition.
- **Infections or toxins** add pressure.
- **Stress and trauma** push harder.
- **Lifestyle patterns** like poor sleep, processed foods, or constant overwork make the load heavier.

When the scale tips, autoimmunity can emerge. But here's the hope: **healing doesn't mean removing every single weight**. It means learning to lighten the load, rebalance the scale, and give your system the chance to reset.

A Patient's Story

"I thought I was losing my mind."
Sonia, age 32, went from doctor to doctor with exhaustion, stomach pain, and brain fog. One told her she was stressed. Another said she should "try yoga." Bloodwork kept coming back "normal." After three years, she was finally diagnosed with celiac disease. Cutting out gluten didn't fix everything overnight, but it gave her clarity, and that clarity was healing.

Like Sonia, many people feel trapped in the space between **"something is wrong"** and **"no one believes me."** The moment of diagnosis can be scary, but it can also be validating: a reminder that you weren't imagining it.

Myths vs. Truths

- **Myth:** "If labs are normal, it's in your head."
  Truth: Autoimmunity can take years to show up on tests. Symptoms often come first.
- **Myth:** "Stress doesn't affect your body."
  Truth: Stress is biology. Hormones and immune messengers shift when you're under pressure, which can fuel flares.
- **Myth:** "Nothing can be done."
  Truth: While there is no single cure, there are many ways to reduce flares, improve quality of life, and reclaim balance.

Healing Is Layered

Autoimmunity doesn't happen overnight, and neither does healing. Balance is built step by step.

- **Medical care** (medications, labs, procedures) addresses inflammation and prevents damage.

- **Lifestyle care** (nutrition, sleep, stress management) reduces triggers and supports resilience.
- **Emotional care** (processing trauma, building support systems) calms the nervous system and allows the immune system to breathe.

You don't have to fix everything at once. Each step lightens the load on your scale.

Reflection & Worksheets

Reflection Questions

- What symptoms first alerted me that something was wrong?
- How do my flares tend to show up?
- What triggers seem most consistent in my life?
- Where have I noticed even small improvements when I change habits or routines?
- Who in my life validates what I'm experiencing, and who dismisses it?

Mini Exercise: My Symptom Map

Draw a simple outline of your body. Mark the areas where you feel symptoms most often (pain, fatigue, rashes, numbness, etc.). Over time, look for patterns. Sometimes visualizing it helps make sense of what feels random.

Key Takeaways

- Autoimmunity = mistaken identity, where the immune system targets the self.
- Symptoms often mimic other conditions, leading to long delays in diagnosis.
- There are 80+ autoimmune diseases, each unique but linked by immune misfire.
- Autoimmune thyroid conditions can drive both **underactivity (Hashimoto's)** and **overactivity (Graves')**.
- Think in layers: genetics, infections, stress, lifestyle, and trauma all interact.
- Healing begins with validation, awareness, and learning to rebalance the scale.

Chapter 2

Stress & Emotions: The Biology of Being Overwhelmed

Stress is not just in your mind; it's in your bloodstream, hormones, and immune system. When something unsettles you, whether it's a work deadline or an unresolved conflict, your body can't always tell the difference between *"I'm late for a meeting"* and *"I'm being chased by a bear."*

That's because the stress response is ancient. It starts deep in the brain, in the hypothalamus, and quickly calls the adrenal glands into action. Within moments, adrenaline and cortisol surge through your system. Your heart races, muscles tense, digestion slows, and blood sugar rises. This response is lifesaving if you need to run, fight, or survive.

But when stress never ends, when it's bills, caregiving, unprocessed trauma, or daily micro-pressures, the system doesn't turn off. Cortisol stays high, your immune system loses balance, and inflammation smolders like an unchecked fire. For people with autoimmunity, this creates the perfect storm: **a confused immune system that is already prone to misfiring now faces constant fuel for the fire.**

Emotions as Signals

We're taught to treat emotions as optional things we should "control" or "get over." But in truth, emotions are **biochemical messengers**.

- **Anger** elevates heart rate and muscle tension, spiking pro-inflammatory chemicals.
- **Fear and anxiety** keep cortisol on repeat, preventing repair.
- **Grief** can weaken immune resilience, leaving the body more vulnerable.
- **Joy, laughter, and connection** release oxytocin and endorphins, calming the nervous system and cooling inflammation.

Ignoring emotions doesn't make them disappear; it drives them deeper, where they often surface as physical symptoms.

The Weight of Suppression

Many with autoimmunity share a familiar story: growing up in environments where emotions were unsafe or unwelcome.

- Being told, *"Don't cry, toughen up."*
- Learning that expressing feelings = rejection or conflict.
- Taking on the role of caregiver, while never voicing their own needs.

This emotional backlog keeps the nervous system on constant alert, as though danger is always around the corner. Over time, the immune system interprets that "danger" as a reason to stay activated.

Stress, Symptoms, and Body Signals

Stress doesn't just sit in your mind; it **lands in your body**, often in predictable places. Each area of the body carries its own vulnerabilities when stress lingers too long. Pairing medical science with energy awareness gives a fuller picture.

- **Head / Crown (Crown Chakra imbalance)**
    - Symptoms: headaches, migraines, and brain fog.
    - Stress link: mental overload, feeling disconnected from purpose or spirituality.
    - Reset: grounding rituals, meditation, quiet reflection.
- **Throat / Neck (Throat Chakra)**
    - Symptoms: tight throat, frequent sore throats, thyroid imbalance, tension in the shoulders.
    - Stress link: feeling unheard, suppressing truth, "swallowing" emotions.

- o Reset: journaling unspoken words, gentle neck stretches, humming or singing to release.
- **Chest / Heart (Heart Chakra)**
  - o Symptoms: palpitations, chest tightness, shortness of breath, shallow breathing.
  - o Stress link: grief, loss, betrayal, or lack of safe connection.
  - o Reset: deep breathing, safe touch/hugs, gratitude practices.
- **Digestive System / Gut (Solar Plexus + Sacral)**
  - o Symptoms: nausea, IBS, bloating, cramps.
  - o Stress link: "gut feelings" ignored, fear of instability, difficulty processing experiences.
  - o Reset: mindful eating, probiotics/anti-inflammatory foods, belly breathing.
- **Reproductive / Lower Back / Hips (Sacral & Root)**
  - o Symptoms: cramps, pelvic pain, low back tension, irregular cycles.

- - Stress link: insecurity, blocked creativity, financial strain, fear of survival.
  - Reset: hip-opening stretches, grounding movement (walking, dancing), affirmations of safety and belonging.
- **Muscles & Joints (Root & Sacral grounding)**
  - Symptoms: chronic aches, stiffness, fatigue.
  - Stress link: carrying burdens, "holding it all together" for others, lack of rest.
  - Reset: rest, massage, supportive movement (yoga, tai chi).

These patterns are not random. They are the body's way of pointing to imbalance, an invitation to listen instead of ignoring.

Tools for Releasing Stress and Emotions

1. Journaling
Writing even 5 minutes a day helps translate swirling emotions into words, reducing stress hormones. Prompts might include:

- "Today I feel…"
- "The hardest part of my week was…"
- "One thing I wish someone knew about my health is…"

2. Breathing & Mindfulness
Breathing in for 4, holding for 4, exhaling for 6 activates the vagus nerve, telling the body it's safe. Mindfulness can be as simple as noticing the weight of your feet on the ground.

3. Reframing Thoughts
Instead of "I failed," try "I learned something about my limits." Reframing lightens the emotional weight without denying the struggle.

4. Safe Expression

- Talking to a trusted friend or therapist.
- Moving anger out physically (punching a pillow, exercise).
- Allowing grief through crying, art, or rituals.

5. Micro-Joys

Moments of joy are medicine: sunlight, laughter, favorite songs, a short walk. They don't erase stress, but they remind the nervous system of safety.

A Patient's Story

Carla, 36, struggled with lupus flares that seemed random. Through journaling, she noticed they coincided with family conflicts and work deadlines. By adding nightly breathing practices and learning to set firmer boundaries, her flares didn't disappear, but they became less frequent and less severe. She learned that caring for her emotions was as important as her medication.

Reflection & Worksheets

Reflection Questions

- How does my body signal stress? (jaw tension, stomach knots, headaches?)
- What practices help me reset in under 5 minutes?
- Which emotion do I avoid most, and how could I face it gently?
- Where in my body do I most often feel stress, and what might that area represent emotionally?

Mini Stress Log (1 week)

Track: Situation | Emotion | Physical feeling | Stress 0–10 | Reset used | Result

Key Takeaways

- Stress is not weakness; it's biology.
- Chronic stress causes cortisol resistance and inflammation.
- Emotions are chemical messengers that directly shape immunity.
- Suppressing emotions adds weight to the body's stress load.
- Symptoms often cluster in specific body zones, linking biology with energy imbalance.
- Daily practices: journaling, breathing, reframing, safe expression, joy, reducing that weight, and creating room for healing.

Chapter 3

Trauma, Triggers, and the Body

Autoimmune conditions are not only influenced by genetics, but also environmental trauma plays a significant role. Trauma can be emotional, physical, or a combination of both. Whether from childhood experiences, complex relationships, or even life-threatening events, trauma leaves imprints on the nervous system. Over time, these imprints can disrupt immune regulation and contribute to autoimmune flares.

Many people associate trauma only with extreme events such as war, natural disasters, or physical assault. While these certainly count, trauma also includes experiences that overwhelm a person's ability to cope with bullying, neglect, chronic stress, betrayal, or growing up in unsafe or unstable homes. The body doesn't distinguish between "big" or "small" trauma; it registers all of it as stress.

The Nervous System's Role

When trauma occurs, the nervous system shifts into survival mode. The body releases cortisol and adrenaline, preparing to fight, flee, or freeze. If the trauma is unresolved, this stress response can remain "switched on." Over time, chronic stress contributes to:

- Inflammation throughout the body.
- Dysregulation of the thyroid and adrenal glands.
- Gut imbalances, including irritable bowel and food sensitivities.
- Hormonal shifts that increase autoimmune vulnerability.
- Flare-ups of conditions like lupus, multiple sclerosis, or rheumatoid arthritis.

Attachment, Belonging & Immune Safety

When we feel safely attached to a caregiver, partner, friend, or community, the nervous system learns, *"I'm held."* That message is biochemical: oxytocin rises, heart rate variability improves, and inflammatory signals quiet.

But when attachment is inconsistent or unsafe, the body learns to be vigilant. Muscles brace, breath shortens, digestion stalls, and the immune system hovers near "ready to react."

Attachment patterns often show up in health:

- **Anxious attachment** - scanning for rejection; flares during conflict or uncertainty.
- **Avoidant attachment** - downplaying needs; flares after long periods of pushing through without rest.
- **Disorganized attachment** - wanting closeness but fearing it; flares around intimacy or significant life changes.

Healing doesn't require perfect relationships; it requires *reliable enough* signals of safety. That can be a consistent bedtime, a weekly call with a trusted friend, prayer or meditation before sleep, or therapy with a supportive provider. Each "I'm safe right now" moment establishes a new baseline for your immune system.

Micro-Practices to Rebuild Safety

- **Co-regulation minute**: sit with someone you trust, match breathing for 60 seconds.
- **Safety statement**: hand to chest, "In this moment, I am safe. My body can soften."
- **Belonging scan**: list 3 places or people who make you feel welcome.
- **Body boundary**: 5-minute stretch focusing on shoulders, jaw, and hips, typical "armor zones."

How Trauma Shows Up in the Body

Emotional Trauma

People raised in environments where their feelings were dismissed or unsafe often carry high baseline stress into adulthood. This is sometimes referred to as **toxic stress**.

Examples include:

- Childhood abuse, neglect, or exposure to violence.
- Repeated rejection, abandonment, or betrayal.
- Living with unpredictable caregivers or unstable environments.
- Being silenced, shamed, or made to suppress self-expression.

These experiences create lasting changes in the **hypothalamic-pituitary-adrenal (HPA) axis**, the body's stress-regulation system. When disrupted, the immune system becomes hypersensitive, increasing the risk of autoimmune conditions.

Physical Trauma

Physical injury or assaults may also affect specific body systems. For example, trauma to the neck (such as strangulation, whiplash, or surgery) can influence thyroid function and vagus nerve signaling. For someone genetically predisposed, this physical stress can be enough to trigger or worsen autoimmune conditions.

Medical Trauma & Advocacy

Medical settings can retraumatize with bright lights, rushed visits, and not being believed. Planning restores agency and reduces flares.

Before the Appointment

- Write the top **3 concerns** and **1 clear ask** (e.g., "Full thyroid panel incl. antibodies").
- Bring a **flare log** (dates, triggers, symptoms, what helped).
- Choose a **support person** or ask to record (if allowed).

During the Appointment Script Starters

- "My symptoms flare with stress and sleep loss. I'd like to **rule in or out** thyroid and autoimmune markers."
- "When I'm dismissed, my care stalls. Can we **document** today's plan and next steps?"

- "I need a moment to regulate. Can we pause for a slow breath?"

After the Appointment

- Get the visit summary and **copies of labs**.
- Note **follow-ups** with dates.
- If minimized or dismissed, consider a second opinion (endocrinology, rheumatology, GI, or integrative).

Tests to Ask About (tailor to your history)

- **Autoimmune screen**: ANA, CRP/ESR.
- **Thyroid**: TSH, Free T3, Free T4, TPO/Tg antibodies.
- **Metabolic/hormones**: A1C, fasting insulin, Vitamin D, B12, ferritin; sex hormones as appropriate.
- **GI (if indicated)**: celiac panel; stool tests for inflammation.

PTSD Reframed

PTSD isn't just about combat. Trauma can arise from:

- Childbirth complications.
- Car accidents.
- Invasive surgeries.
- Chronic caregiving stress.
- Emotional neglect or betrayal.

Framing PTSD as *"post-traumatic stress"* rather than a disorder helps normalize the experience. It reminds readers that the body is reacting to something real, not "overreacting" or "broken."

Trauma Triggers in Adulthood

Even if the original trauma happened years ago, certain triggers in adulthood can reactivate the stress response. These may include:

- Stressful jobs or relationships.
- Financial insecurity.

- Physical reminders of past trauma (smells, sounds, anniversaries).
- Major life changes such as childbirth, divorce, or loss.

Each trigger may not cause disease directly, but together they can fuel chronic inflammation and immune dysfunction.

Chakras and Emotional Blockages

Energy systems reflect physical patterns.

- **Throat Chakra**: expression, truth, boundaries. Trauma here may manifest as thyroid imbalance or chronic sore throats.
- **Solar Plexus Chakra**: personal power and identity. Imbalances can show as digestive distress or low energy.
- **Heart Chakra**: love, connection, grief. Wounds here may influence breathing, chest tightness, or immune suppression.

Balancing practices (affirmations, meditation, gentle yoga) help restore flow where trauma created blockages.

Stories of Real People

Tanya, 33, developed Hashimoto's after years of being silenced in a toxic marriage. She later realized her symptoms flared whenever she felt unable to speak her truth.

James, 40, survived a car accident that left him with chronic back pain. Over time, he also developed rheumatoid arthritis. He believes the accident "lit the fuse" for a condition already in his genes.

Nia, 28, grew up with unpredictable caregivers. As an adult, she developed Crohn's disease. Learning about toxic stress helped her understand why her gut seemed to "remember" the chaos.

Vagus Nerve Reset Toolkit (7-Day Plan)

Your vagus nerve is the body's brake pedal. Training it daily builds calm, improves digestion and sleep, and lowers inflammation.

Five Core Techniques (2–5 minutes each)

1. 4-4-6 breath (in 4, hold 4, out 6).
2. Humming/chanting.
3. Cold splash or cool pack on neck.
4. Gaze softening (peripheral vision for 60–90 sec).
5. Legs-up-wall (2–5 minutes).

7-Day Rotation

- Mon: 4-4-6 breath + humming.
- Tue: Legs-up-wall.
- Wed: Cold splash + smile.
- Thu: Gaze softening + gratitude note.
- Fri: Breath before difficult tasks.
- Sat: Nature walk.
- Sun: Gentle stretch + long exhale.

Healing Pathways

Healing trauma is not about erasing the past but learning how to live with resilience in the present. This includes:

- **Therapy**: trauma-informed therapy, EMDR, somatic experiencing.
- **Mind-Body Practices**: meditation, yoga, tai chi, breathwork.
- **Bodywork**: massage, craniosacral therapy, acupuncture.
- **Community Support**: safe relationships and peer groups.

Caregiver Corner & Partner Support

Autoimmunity and trauma ripple through households. Caregivers need a map too.

What Helps

- Predictable rhythms (mealtimes, bedtime).

- Choice language: "Do you want a walk or legs-up-wall?"
- Validation: "I believe you. How can I support you right now?"
- Repair after conflict: apology + plan ("Next time I'll listen first").

Reflection & Worksheets

Reflection Questions

- What early experiences shaped how I handle stress today?
- Do I notice certain situations or people triggering physical symptoms?
- How does my body respond when I feel unsafe, tension, pain, fatigue?
- What coping strategies have I used that help, and which ones hold me back?

Grounding Exercise: The 5–4–3–2–1 Method

When triggered, pause and name:

- 5 things you see
- 4 things you feel (touch)
- 3 things you hear
- 2 things you smell
- 1 thing you taste

Mini Reset for Flare Days

- Step 1: Breathe slowly in for 4 counts, out for 6.
- Step 2: Place your hand on the tense area: "I hear you."
- Step 3: Move gently (stretch, walk, sway).

Journaling Prompt

- Write about a time you felt unsafe but survived. What strengths or lessons did you carry forward?

Partner Script

- "When flares hit, I'll handle dinner. Let's make a flare plan on the fridge."
- "If an appointment feels overwhelming, I can come, take notes, and ask your questions."

Key Takeaways

- Trauma can be both emotional and physical, and both influence immune regulation.
- The nervous system translates trauma into inflammation and autoimmune flares.
- Physical trauma (like neck injuries) may impact organ function and immune balance.
- Emotional trauma reshapes stress pathways and can linger for decades.
- Healing involves both body and mind therapy, movement, grounding, and safe relationships.
- Caregivers and partners can play a healing role when equipped with tools and scripts.
- Reflection and exercises give practical ways to manage triggers and reclaim safety.

Chapter 4

Reproductive Health and Hidden Diagnoses

Reproductive health is often treated as separate from overall health, as though cycles, hormones, or fertility exist in isolation from the rest of the body. But for many people with autoimmune conditions, reproductive health is one of the first places symptoms appear. Pain, irregular cycles, fatigue, and inflammation often get misattributed to "just hormones," delaying proper diagnosis and leaving people confused and unsupported.

The truth is this: reproductive health is deeply tied to immune function. Hormones interact with inflammation, stress, and emotional well-being. When the reproductive system is out of balance, the immune system often is too.

Women's Health and Autoimmunity

Conditions like **endometriosis, PCOS (polycystic ovarian syndrome), uterine fibroids, and ovarian**

cysts are common yet misunderstood. They bring pain, fatigue, and irregular cycles symptoms that overlap with autoimmune flares.

- **Endometriosis**: tissue similar to the uterine lining grows outside the uterus, leading to inflammation, scarring, and immune confusion. It often mimics autoimmune disorders and is highly correlated with immune dysfunction.
- **PCOS**: marked by irregular cycles, insulin resistance, and hormonal imbalance. Chronic inflammation is a common thread.
- **Fibroids and ovarian cysts**: though often dismissed as "benign," they contribute to pain, pressure, and immune stress.

Hormonal transitions, including puberty, pregnancy, postpartum, and menopause, also influence autoimmune activity. Shifts in **estrogen and progesterone** can sometimes protect against flares, while at other times worsen them. Many women first notice autoimmune symptoms during these transitions, yet too often their concerns are minimized as "just hormones."

Men's Health and Autoimmunity

Autoimmune conditions affect more women than men, but men are not immune. In fact, male reproductive health and hormones play a quiet yet powerful role in autoimmunity.

- **Testosterone** generally calms immune activation. Men with chronically low testosterone (from stress, aging, obesity, or medical conditions) face higher risks of conditions like rheumatoid arthritis and lupus.
- **Estrogen balance in men** also matters. Elevated estrogen (relative to testosterone) may worsen immune dysregulation.
- **Prostate inflammation** (prostatitis) can overlap with immune dysfunction, sometimes misdiagnosed or ignored.

- **Fertility issues** can sometimes trace back to immune-related causes, showing how intertwined reproduction and immunity really are.

Emotional Blockages in Men

Beyond hormones, cultural expectations weigh heavily on men. Many are taught to suppress vulnerability, emotions, or intimacy. This suppression often creates **blockages in the sacral and root chakras**, which can manifest as:

- Sexual dysfunction or low libido.
- Pelvic tension or chronic prostatitis.
- Fatigue and mood imbalance from emotional stagnation.

Some men turn to **semen retention** as a spiritual or lifestyle practice. When used intentionally, it may increase awareness and discipline. But if paired with shame, repression, or secrecy, it can create emotional and energetic stagnation, again stressing the sacral/root balance.

Non-Binary & Trans Perspectives

For those who are non-binary or transgender, hormone therapy (estrogen, testosterone, or hormone blockers) can influence the immune system in significant ways. These shifts may impact inflammation, cycles, fertility, and long-term health. While every individual's journey is unique, the takeaway is universal: **hormones and immunity are inseparable.**

Regardless of gender identity, the body's DNA and genetic makeup set a baseline for immune response. Hormonal support or transition care overlays this baseline, requiring awareness, medical support, and self-care to manage symptoms effectively.

The Silence Around Reproductive Health

One of the most significant barriers to healing is silence. Too many people grow up with the message that reproductive pain is "normal," that cycles should be endured quietly, or that men's struggles with libido or prostate health are signs of weakness. This silence leaves people suffering in isolation, questioning themselves, or feeling ashamed.

The reality is that reproductive health is inseparable from mental, emotional, and physical well-being. When the reproductive system struggles, the immune system often raises its hand too.

Chakras and Reproductive Energy

The **Root Chakra** (base of the spine) governs safety, stability, and survival. When out of balance, it may show up as:

- Low back pain, pelvic tension, or reproductive disorders.
- Anxiety, financial insecurity, or lack of grounding.
- A sense of disconnection from one's body or environment.

The **Sacral Chakra** (lower abdomen) governs sexuality, creativity, and reproductive energy. Imbalances often appear as:

- Irregular cycles, pelvic pain, or infertility struggles.
- Low libido, shame around sexuality, or creative blockages.
- Emotional stagnation or lack of pleasure in life.

Balancing these chakras supports both physical and emotional health. Practices include:

- Grounding exercises (walking barefoot, meditation focused on safety and belonging).
- Pelvic or hip-opening stretches to release tension.
- Creative expression (art, dance, writing) to reawaken flow.
- Affirmations such as *"I am safe in my body"* or *"I honor my creative and sexual energy."*

Stories of Real People

Sophia, 31, struggled for years with painful periods and fatigue. Doctors brushed it off as "just cramps" until she was finally diagnosed with endometriosis. She later discovered that her flares worsened during stressful work seasons. Learning relaxation practices and seeking trauma-informed gynecological care gave her back some control.

Marcus, 40, experienced low libido and chronic pelvic pain. He resisted opening up about it, believing it made him "less of a man." Eventually, he learned his symptoms were tied to both low testosterone and unresolved emotional stress. Therapy, hormone support, and grounding practices improved his energy and immune resilience.

Amira, 27, began gender-affirming hormone therapy as part of their transition. Alongside emotional relief, they noticed shifts in cycle patterns and flare intensity. Working closely with supportive providers allowed them to track both hormone and immune changes, making care more proactive and affirming.

Healing Approaches

- **Medical Care** - gynecological/urological evaluation, hormone testing, autoimmune labs.
- **Endocrinology** - An endocrinologist can evaluate thyroid, adrenal, and reproductive hormone balance. They are a key partner when fatigue, mood shifts, or unexplained reproductive changes persist.
- **Lifestyle Care** - anti-inflammatory nutrition, rest, gentle exercise, stress management.
- **Bodywork** - pelvic floor therapy, massage, yoga for hips and spine.
- **Emotional Support** - therapy, safe conversations, breaking stigma.
- **Energy Practices** - chakra balancing, meditation, creative flow.

Reflection & Worksheets

Reflection Questions

- What reproductive health experiences have shaped how I view my body?
- Have I ever felt dismissed or unheard about pain or cycle changes?
- Do I notice links between stress, emotions, and reproductive symptoms?
- How do I experience energy in my lower body as flow, stagnation, or pain?

Symptom and Cycle Log (1 Month)

- Track cycle changes, pelvic pain, fatigue, or libido shifts.
- Note flares alongside stress levels or emotional events.

Chakra Check-In

- Root: Do I feel safe, grounded, and supported?

- Sacral: Do I feel free to express sexuality, creativity, and joy?
- What practices could I use this week to restore balance?

Key Takeaways

- Reproductive health and immunity are deeply connected.
- Women face conditions like endometriosis, PCOS, and fibroids that overlap with autoimmune flares.
- Men's hormone balance (especially testosterone) influences autoimmune risk, and emotional suppression often worsens symptoms.
- Non-binary and trans individuals may experience unique immune shifts during hormone therapy.
- Silence and stigma delay diagnosis. Open conversations are essential.
- Endocrinologists play a key role in evaluating hormone and immune overlap.
- Root and Sacral chakra imbalances often mirror reproductive and immune struggles, and balancing practices can support healing.

Chapter 5

Genetics, Environment & Early Development

Autoimmune conditions don't arise from a single cause. Instead, they develop through a mix of inherited tendencies, environmental triggers, and early life influences. Together, these layers create either resilience or vulnerability.

Understanding the interplay between what we inherit and what we experience helps explain why some people develop autoimmune conditions while others with similar genes do not.

The Genetic Blueprint

Genes create the foundation of how the immune system functions, but they are not fixed outcomes. Having a parent, sibling, or grandparent with an autoimmune condition increases risk, but it doesn't guarantee you will develop one yourself.

For example:

- A grandmother with rheumatoid arthritis may have a daughter with thyroid disease and a grandson with psoriasis.
- The underlying predisposition is the same: immune dysregulation, expressed in different ways.

The difference often lies in what *activates* those genes.

Epigenetics: Genes in Motion

Epigenetics shows us that genes are like piano keys. The environment is the sheet music, it determines which keys are played and which stay silent.

- Chronic stress, trauma, or toxin exposure may "switch on" inflammatory genes.
- Nutrition, supportive community, and stress regulation may "silence" harmful pathways.

- Even reframing the mindset to reduce stress and practicing forgiveness can reduce the impact of genetic vulnerabilities.

This doesn't erase genetics, but it shows how daily choices shape gene expression across a lifetime.

Environmental Triggers

While genes provide the blueprint, the environment writes the story. Autoimmune conditions often develop when multiple triggers overlap, creating a "perfect storm."

Common Triggers Include:

- **Infections**: viruses, bacteria, or chronic illness that push the immune system into overdrive.
- **Toxins**: mold, heavy metals, pesticides, or secondhand smoke.
- **Stress**: unresolved trauma, caregiving burdens, or financial insecurity.

- **Lifestyle**: poor sleep, highly processed diets, or lack of movement.

Each factor adds weight. A single trigger may not be enough, but several stacked together can overwhelm the immune system.

Pregnancy & Early Development

Immune health doesn't begin in adulthood. In many cases, the seeds are planted before birth. Pregnancy creates a unique environment where nutrition, stress, and exposures influence how a child's immune system develops.

Nutrition & Food Preferences

- Flavors from the mother's diet pass into amniotic fluid and breast milk.
- Babies exposed to certain foods in utero may crave them later; others may resist what was absent.

- Example: a pregnancy rich in vegetables may lead to openness to greens, while one heavy in fried foods may predispose cravings for the same.

Stress & Mood

- Stress hormones like cortisol cross the placenta. High maternal stress may prime children to be more reactive to stress later in life.
- Joy, prayer, laughter, and calm during pregnancy can help regulate fetal nervous system development.
- Parents often notice echoes of pregnancy moods in children's personalities; a tense pregnancy may reflect in anxious tendencies; a calmer one in steadier temperaments.

Immune Shifts & Skin Conditions

- Autoimmune flares, rashes, or eczema in pregnancy may sometimes predict sensitivities in children.

- These aren't guarantees but offer clues about immune tendencies.

Substances & Exposures

- **Alcohol** - increases risk for asthma, allergies, immune weakness, and developmental issues.
- **Drugs (opioids, cocaine, or misused prescriptions)** - disrupt nervous and immune system development.
- **Smoking & vaping** - reduce oxygen and increase autoimmune risk.
- **Secondhand smoke, toxins, or chemicals** - heavy metals, pesticides, and fumes can affect fetal immunity.

Key Insight:
Pregnancy isn't about perfection. No one can control every factor, and parents are not to blame for conditions outside their power. Awareness gives families more tools to support long-term health.

The Interplay of Body, Mind & Spirit

Autoimmunity is never just physical. Stress, trauma, and unexpressed emotions influence how genes and the immune system are expressed. Childhood adversity or blocked emotional expression may become embodied as thyroid imbalance, gut issues, or chronic inflammation.

When we address both the biological and emotional roots, the body finds more space for balance.

Reflection & Worksheets

Reflection Questions

- What autoimmune conditions run in my family?
- Which environmental factors (stress, toxins, lifestyle) affect me most today?
- What do I know about my mother's pregnancy with me? Are there clues that connect to my current health?
- Where might my emotional stress be fueling genetic tendencies?

Worksheet: Mapping My Story

- **Family history** - list autoimmune conditions across generations.
- **Environmental triggers** - infections, toxins, stressors that may connect to symptoms.
- **Pregnancy/early life** - diet, stress, or exposures you're aware of.

Personal stress inventory - highlight areas of unresolved trauma or overcommitment.

Key Takeaways

- Genes set the blueprint, but the environment determines activation.
- Epigenetics explains why stress, diet, and trauma can "switch on" or silence disease pathways.
- Autoimmunity often appears across generations, but in different forms.
- Pregnancy and early development shape immune tendencies through nutrition, mood, and exposures.
- Emotional and spiritual well-being influence how genetic risk plays out in daily life.

CHAPTER 6

Conception, Surrogacy & Immune Beginnings

Health doesn't begin at birth. From the very moment of conception, the **first roots of immunity** are already being laid. The health of the parents, the environment of the pregnancy, and even the emotions carried during those nine months all leave impressions. These influences don't dictate fate, but they shape foundations. Some children begin life with greater resilience, others with vulnerabilities, not out of chance but because health begins as a layered story long before symptoms appear.

Conception

The condition of the egg and sperm at conception sets the earliest blueprint. Alcohol, drugs, toxins, and even prolonged stress in either parent can disrupt genetic stability. This is why certain developmental issues, such as neural tube defects or nervous system sensitivities, are linked to exposures during conception.

Science shows sperm quality changes with lifestyle: smoking, heavy drinking, and poor nutrition damage DNA. Eggs are also affected by age, hormonal balance, and maternal health. These realities aren't about perfection; they're about awareness. Even small changes before conception can have long-term effects on a child's health.

Surrogacy

Surrogacy reminds us that the womb is not a passive container. The surrogate's body supplies oxygen, hormones, immune signals, and nutrients that interact with the fetus. If the surrogate experiences illness, high stress, or poor nutrition, those conditions may echo in the child. On the other hand, when the surrogate is supported and healthy, resilience is strengthened.

Real-World Note: One mother developed cancer during pregnancy. The treatments necessary to save her life inevitably influenced the developing baby. Though rare, these situations highlight how closely a parent's health is linked to the womb environment. These stories are not meant to create fear, but to bring compassion. Pregnancy is never simple biology; it is life circumstances, challenges, and resilience all woven together.

Emotional Imprints

Pregnancy health is not only physical, but also emotional. Cortisol and other stress hormones cross the placenta, priming the baby's nervous system. A pregnancy filled with conflict, grief, or financial worry may leave the child more sensitive to stress later in life. A pregnancy filled with calm, prayer, or joy may strengthen resilience.

From an energy perspective, pregnancy aligns with the chakra system.

- Root and Sacral imbalances in the parent may echo as insecurity or digestive sensitivities.
- Solar Plexus stress may show up as gut reactivity or emotional volatility in children.
- Heart and Throat imprints may influence how children later express emotions or build safe connections.

These imprints are not life sentences. With love, therapy, community, and conscious healing, they can be reshaped.

Generational Echoes

Health during pregnancy doesn't only reflect one lifetime. Epigenetics shows us that grandparents' trauma, toxins, or stress can echo down through generations. This is why certain conditions "run in families" even when lifestyles differ. Genes are not fixed; they are turned on or off by the environment. Just as trauma can leave marks, healing practices can switch resilience pathways back on.

Reflection & Worksheets

Reflection Questions

- What do I know about my own conception or pregnancy story?
- How might my parents' health, stress, or exposures have influenced my beginnings?
- If I've been pregnant, what echoes of that experience do I notice in my child?
- Where can I let go of guilt and focus on supportive steps today?

Early Health Mapping Log

Use this log to reflect on early influences and how they might connect to health now.

Factor	What I Know	Possible Echo	Supportive Practice
Conception (parent stress, substances, illness)			
Pregnancy (nutrition, mood, exposures)			
Birth/Early Life (delivery, antibiotics, feeding)			

Key Takeaways

- Conception health matters: egg and sperm quality influence early nervous system and immune patterns.
- The womb environment is active, and surrogate health, parental illness, and pregnancy exposures all leave imprints.
- Emotional states during pregnancy can prime children's stress responses, but resilience can be cultivated later.
- Generational echoes remind us that health patterns can cross generations, but so can healing.
- Awareness is empowering, not blaming. Every supportive step builds stronger foundations.

Chapter 7

Blood Type Health & Genetics

When it comes to autoimmunity, no two bodies respond in the same way. One person may develop thyroid issues, another may battle joint pain, and another may face digestive flares. Why? Part of the answer lies in **blood type and genetics**.

Blood type and genetic background don't determine your future completely, but they shape how your immune system reacts to stress, infections, and inflammation. Knowing your body's natural tendencies can help you make choices that reduce risk and strengthen resilience.

Blood Type and Immunity

Your blood type is more than just a label for transfusions. The proteins (antigens) on your red blood cells influence how your immune system recognizes "self" and "other." These subtle differences can affect disease risk.

- **Type O**
    - Often considered more resistant to certain infections.
    - Some studies suggest a lower risk of blood-clotting disorders.
    - May be at higher risk of ulcers or digestive issues.
    - Tends to mount strong immune responses that are protective in some ways, but overactive in others.
- **Type A**
    - Associated with higher levels of cortisol in stressful situations.
    - May have an increased risk for cardiovascular disease and certain autoimmune conditions.
    - Often sensitive to stress-related digestive issues.
- **Type B**
    - Shows more balanced immune responses in some research.

- o Linked to both protective and risk factors depending on the condition.
- o May face a higher risk for certain infections.
- **Type AB**
  - o Rare, with a mix of traits from A and B.
  - o May carry unique risks for cardiovascular and clotting issues.
  - o Some studies suggest greater vulnerability to stress-related inflammation.

Important: These are *patterns*, not predictions. Blood type is one piece of the puzzle, not a verdict.

Genetics and Autoimmunity

Autoimmune conditions tend to run in families. Specific gene variations, especially **HLA (human leukocyte antigen) markers**, are known to increase susceptibility. For example:

- **HLA-DR and HLA-DQ** variants are linked to type 1 diabetes, celiac disease, and thyroid disorders.
- **HLA-B27** is strongly associated with ankylosing spondylitis (a spinal autoimmune condition).
- **Family clustering**: If one relative has lupus, another may be more prone to rheumatoid arthritis or thyroid disease.

Genetics lays a foundation, but it is not destiny.

Epigenetics: The Switches We Control

Epigenetics is the study of how lifestyle and environment influence gene expression. Think of it as a set of "light switches" that can turn tendencies on or off.

- **Stress**: Chronic cortisol can activate inflammatory pathways.
- **Nutrition**: Anti-inflammatory foods can help quiet overactive immune responses.
- **Toxins**: Smoking, alcohol, and chemical exposures may "switch on" vulnerable genes.

- **Healing**: Practices like meditation, breathwork, journaling, and movement can positively influence gene expression.

Real-World Examples

- Meditation has been shown to **down-regulate genes** linked to inflammation.
- Childhood trauma can **upregulate stress genes** that increase disease risk later in life.
- Exercise can **reprogram gene activity** to improve immunity and reduce chronic inflammation.

In other words, your DNA loads the gun, but lifestyle pulls (or avoids pulling) the trigger.

Blood Conditions Beyond Autoimmunity: The Case of Sickle Cell

Not all blood-related conditions are autoimmune. Some, like **sickle cell disease (SCD)**, are purely genetic, but they carry lessons that resonate with anyone managing chronic health struggles.

- **What it is** - SCD is caused by a genetic mutation that changes the shape of red blood cells. Instead of smooth, round disks, the cells are rigid and crescent shaped. This leads to blockages in blood flow, chronic pain crises, anemia, and a higher risk of organ damage and infections.
- **Inheritance** - Sickle cell occurs when a child inherits the gene from both parents. Carrying only one copy (the "trait") usually causes mild or no illness, but under extreme stress (dehydration, altitude, illness), even carriers can face complications.
- **Prevalence** - SCD is most common in people of **African descent**, but it also affects those with ancestry from the **Mediterranean, Middle East, India, and Caribbean regions**. In the U.S., about 1 in 365 African American babies is born with SCD, and 1 in 13 carries the trait.

- **Connection to immunity** - While not autoimmune, the constant stress and inflammation caused by sickled cells mimic aspects of immune dysfunction. Many with SCD also face a heightened risk of infections, requiring lifelong care and monitoring.

Why it matters here: SCD is a powerful reminder that genetics matter, but compassion, awareness, and proactive care are equally important. It also honors those living and those we've lost to genetic conditions that demand strength and resilience every day.

Ancestry and Autoimmune Patterns

Certain autoimmune conditions show up more often in specific ancestries:

- **Northern European ancestry**: higher risk of multiple sclerosis (MS).
- **Ashkenazi Jewish ancestry**: increased risk of Crohn's disease and inflammatory bowel disorders.

- **African ancestry**: higher risk of lupus and certain thyroid conditions.
- **Asian ancestry**: unique autoimmune presentations, such as Behçet's disease.

This doesn't mean any group is "doomed," but awareness allows for early screening and prevention.

Trauma as a Trigger

Genetics creates vulnerability, but trauma can act as the "switch" that activates illness.

- **Physical trauma**: Injuries or assaults in specific body areas may later influence autoimmune activity. For example, trauma to the neck (whiplash, strangulation, surgery) can affect thyroid function.
- **Emotional trauma**: Chronic stress or abuse reshapes the nervous system and immune activity, increasing disease risk.
- **Combination**: Family history + trauma = a more powerful setup for autoimmune conditions.

This explains why two people with the same genetic markers may have very different outcomes: one develops the disease, the other does not.

Family History: Learning from Patterns

Understanding your family's health history can be empowering, not scary. It allows you to:

- Look for repeating patterns of autoimmunity, reproductive health struggles, or chronic illness.
- Take proactive steps if multiple relatives share conditions (like thyroid disease or arthritis).
- Open conversations about health that break cycles of silence.

Blood Type & Health Chart

Blood Type	Potential Strengths	Potential Risks	Lifestyle Tips
O	Strong immune response, lower clotting risk	Ulcers, digestive stress	Balanced meals, stress relief, gut support
A	Adaptable, good with structure	Stress sensitivity, thyroid risk	Mind-body practices, anti-inflammatory foods
B	Balanced immunity	Certain infections, inflammation	Consistency, hydration, immune-friendly diet
AB	Flexible traits	Stress-related inflammation, clotting issues	Stress reduction, circulation support,

Stories of Real People

Lena, 29, learned she was type A after years of digestive struggles. When she discovered the link between stress, cortisol, and her blood type tendencies, she began integrating yoga and meditation into her routine. Her flares didn't vanish, but her recovery time shortened.

Diego, 42, had a family history of rheumatoid arthritis. Though he had no diagnosis yet, he noticed recurring joint stiffness. By asking for genetic testing and tracking inflammation markers early, he began anti-inflammatory nutrition and exercise before symptoms escalated.

Andre, 17, lived with sickle cell disease. He experienced cycles of intense pain that often-interrupted school and social life. Despite this, he found strength in sharing his story, raising awareness, and reminding others that resilience is possible even in the face of lifelong conditions.

Healing Approaches

- **Know your numbers**: learn your blood type, track family health patterns, and request key labs.
- **Endocrinology check-ins**: thyroid and adrenal testing can reveal imbalances tied to both genetics and blood type stress tendencies.
- **Personalized nutrition**: lean into whole foods, anti-inflammatory meals, and foods that feel good for *your* body, not just a trend.
- **Stress management**: since stress flips genetic switches, practices like breathwork, journaling, and meditation are medicine.

Reflection & Worksheets

Reflection Questions

- What do I know about my blood type?
- What patterns of illness exist in my family?
- Do I know anyone with sickle cell or another genetic condition that shaped my perspective on health?
- Have I experienced trauma that might have left lasting marks on my health?
- Which lifestyle shifts feel most accessible right now?

Family Health Map

- Write down relatives and their known conditions.
- Circle any patterns (thyroid, arthritis, reproductive, digestive).
- Consider what steps you can take to support those vulnerable areas in yourself.

Blood Type Journal Prompt

- If my blood type influences how my body responds to stress or food, what might that mean for my daily habits?

Key Takeaways

- Blood type and genetics shape how the immune system responds to stress and inflammation.
- Certain blood types may be linked to higher or lower risks, but they don't define destiny.
- Autoimmune conditions often run in families due to shared genetics and lifestyle.
- Epigenetics shows that stress, trauma, nutrition, and healing practices can turn genes "on" or "off."
- Sickle cell disease is a genetic blood condition that highlights resilience, systemic health challenges, and the need for compassion and proactive care.
- Physical or emotional trauma can activate conditions in people who are already genetically predisposed.
- Understanding your family history, blood type, and potential genetic markers allows for proactive care.

Chapter 8

Supportive Practices & Reframing Stress

Stress is one of the most powerful influences on health and one of the most overlooked. While some stress is natural, constant or unresolved stress keeps the immune system in a heightened state of alert, creating the perfect storm for autoimmune flares, fatigue, and chronic inflammation.

Stress management isn't about "healing" autoimmunity or eliminating every difficulty in life. It's about reducing the **burden stress places on the body**, so your immune system can regulate more effectively. When we change how we relate to stress, symptoms may feel lighter, recovery time can shorten, and daily life becomes more manageable.

How Stress Makes Autoimmunity Worse

Stress affects every system of the body:

- **Immune system** - Excess cortisol increases inflammation and can trigger flares.
- **Hormones** - Stress disrupts thyroid and adrenal balance, worsening fatigue.
- **Digestive system** - Stress reduces gut lining integrity ("leaky gut"), fueling autoimmunity.
- **Sleep** - Stress shortens deep sleep cycles, reducing repair and recovery.

This is why people often notice new or worsening autoimmune symptoms after a season of intense stress. It doesn't mean stress "caused" the disease, but it can **activate genetic tendencies** and amplify existing conditions.

Stress Is Not Your Fault

Many people with autoimmune conditions feel guilt: *"Maybe I'm sick because I couldn't handle stress better."* This is not true.

Stress is inevitable. Illness is not a personal failure. What matters is how we support the body after stress shows up.

Stress tools are not a cure, but they are valuable companions that:

- Reduce the frequency of flares.
- Make symptoms more manageable.
- Improve mood, energy, and quality of life.

Supportive Practices That Help the Body

Mind-Body Approaches

- **Meditation & Breathwork** - Calm the nervous system and lower inflammation markers.

- **Yoga & Tai Chi** - Gentle movement that eases stiffness and supports balance.
- **Visualization** - Guided imagery to shift the body's sense of safety.

Physical Approaches

- **Movement** - Walking, stretching, or swimming helps reduce inflammation without overexertion.
- **Nutrition** - Anti-inflammatory meals (greens, omega-3s, lean proteins) reduce immune triggers.
- **Sleep Routines** - Regular rest restores cortisol balance.

Emotional & Spiritual Approaches

- **Journaling** - Processes unresolved feelings and lowers rumination.
- **Faith & Prayer** - Provide grounding, hope, and connection to something larger.
- **Community** - Sharing experiences reduces isolation and creates accountability.

Reframing Stress: From Burden to Resource

Stressful events can feel crushing, but with reframing, the same experience can be seen differently:

- **Burden**: "This broke me."
- **Reframe**: "This stretched me. I learned what I need and how I can grow."

Reframing doesn't mean ignoring pain. It means finding meaning that reduces stress's grip on the body.

Example

- Burden: "My diagnosis ruined my life."
- Reframe: "My diagnosis helped me discover the importance of rest and care."

Building Your Stress-Relief Toolkit

Not every tool works for everyone, and you don't need to do them all. Think of this as a menu:

- **Quick resets**: deep breaths, humming, stretching.

- **Daily anchors**: morning walks, prayer, journaling.
- **Weekly practices**: yoga class, therapy session, and massage.
- **Safety practices**: grounding exercises, co-regulation with trusted friends.
- **Practical supports**: budgeting tools, time management, and boundary setting.

Pick two or three that feel accessible and begin there.

Partnering with Providers

Supportive practices are not a replacement for medical care. They work best **alongside treatment**, such as:

- Endocrinology for thyroid monitoring.
- Rheumatology for arthritis management.
- GI specialists for digestive autoimmune conditions.
- Integrative providers for nutrition and whole-body support.

Bringing a **stress management plan** to your doctor shows commitment and can help track improvements in labs like cortisol, CRP, or sleep quality.

Reflection & Worksheets

Reflection Questions

- What stressors in my life are unavoidable? Which ones can be reduced?
- How do I view stress as danger, or as energy I can redirect?
- Which supportive practices feel realistic for me right now?

Reframing Journal Exercise

- Write down one difficult event.
- List the pain it caused.
- Write the lessons or strengths it revealed.
- Close with: "This does not define me; I am adapting through it."

Healing Practice Tracker (1 Week)

- Morning: Breathwork or meditation (yes/no).
- Day: Movement/stretch (yes/no).

- Evening: Reflection/journal (yes/no).
- Circle the days you noticed improved energy or fewer symptoms.

Key Takeaways

- Stress does not cause autoimmunity, but it worsens symptoms and flares.
- Managing stress reduces inflammation and gives the immune system space to regulate.
- Reframing stress doesn't erase pain but shifts how much power it holds over the body.
- Practices are supportive, not cures; they complement medical care.
- Building a personalized toolkit creates consistency and resilience.

CHAPTER 9

FINANCIAL INSECURITY & HEALTH

Money stress is more than numbers on a bank statement; it is a physiological load that can weigh on the immune system, nervous system, and whole body. For many people, financial insecurity is a daily trigger that shapes sleep, eating, relationships, and the ability to manage chronic illness. When left unchecked, this stress becomes more than an external problem; it becomes a health condition in its own right.

The Biology of Money Stress

Financial strain triggers the same stress response as physical danger. Bills, debt, and instability keep cortisol and adrenaline circulating. Over time, this wears down the immune system, raises inflammation, and makes the body more vulnerable to flares.

Chronic financial stress is linked to:

- Hypertension and cardiovascular strain
- Depression, anxiety, and sleep disturbance
- Weakened immune defense against infections
- Increased flare frequency in autoimmune conditions

The body doesn't separate "threats," whether it's a looming eviction or a wild animal; the nervous system responds the same way.

Lifestyle Sacrifices

Financial insecurity often forces people into health trade-offs: skipping medications, postponing doctor visits, or relying on cheaper, processed foods. These sacrifices add to the burden, creating a cycle where financial stress worsens health, and worsening health deepens financial strain.

Stories of Real People

Marcus, 41, lived with lupus and often had to choose between paying utility bills and filling prescriptions. He noticed flares became more frequent when he skipped medications, but his financial situation left him trapped.

Tanya, a single mother with multiple sclerosis, shared how rising grocery prices forced her to rely on packaged foods. Her energy and inflammation worsened, leaving her frustrated that her health was dictated by what she could afford, not what she knew was best.

These stories reflect the reality that many face: money stress is health stress.

The Hidden Toll on Families
Financial strain ripples through households. Children raised in high-stress financial environments often carry higher risks of anxiety, obesity, and chronic illness later in life. Partners may experience relationship conflict, and caregivers may burn out faster when financial stress piles on top of health responsibilities.

Breaking the Cycle

While financial realities cannot always be changed quickly, some steps help reduce the health impact.

- Support groups can reduce the isolation that magnifies stress.
- Community resources, such as food pantries, low-cost clinics, or utility assistance, can provide breathing room.
- Building financial literacy and small planning steps, even if imperfect, can restore a sense of control.

Resilience Practices for Financial Stress

- Breathing techniques and mindfulness for immediate stress relief.
- Journaling money worries to get them out of the body and onto paper.
- Setting small, realistic health goals that fit a budget (like daily stretching, walking, or preparing simple anti-inflammatory meals).

- Celebrating progress, even tiny wins, to remind the nervous system that not everything is out of control.

Resources & Tools for Financial Support

Financial stress can feel isolating, but resources do exist. Exploring even one new support can reduce the burden:

- **Medical cost assistance** - Some pharmaceutical companies offer patient assistance programs that lower or cover medication costs. Nonprofit organizations such as the *Patient Advocate Foundation* and *NeedyMeds* provide guidance and resources.
- **Community support** - Food pantries, community gardens, and local wellness programs can help meet nutrition needs without high costs. Many communities also have free or sliding-scale fitness and yoga classes.
- **Government programs** - Medicaid expansion, disability support (SSD/SSI), and utility

assistance programs can provide financial relief. While applying can be stressful, these programs are designed to help.

- **Nonprofit and advocacy groups** - Groups focused on autoimmune conditions often have grants or small funds for patients in crisis. Organizations like the *National Multiple Sclerosis Society* or the *Lupus Foundation of America* offer both financial and emotional support.
- **Mental health resources** - Free or low-cost therapy options exist through hotlines, group programs, or telehealth platforms. Mental health support eases the stress response, even if financial strain remains.

While these supports may not erase financial insecurity, they can create breathing room. Sometimes knowing you're not alone and that help is available shifts the body out of survival mode.

Reflection & Worksheets

Reflection Questions:

- How does financial stress show up in my body (sleep issues, headaches, flare-ups)?
- What sacrifices do I notice myself making when money is tight?
- Which community or personal resources could I lean on more?
- What small, no-cost practices could help me lower stress this week?

Money Stress & Health Log (use as a journal):

- Situation: _____
- Emotion: _____
- Physical symptom: _____
- Stress level (0–10): _____
- Coping strategy used: _____
- Result: _____

Key Takeaways

- Financial stress activates the same biological pathways as physical danger, keeping the body in a state of fight-or-flight.
- Chronic money stress worsens autoimmune flares and overall immune function.
- Lifestyle sacrifices, such as skipping medications or choosing cheaper foods, can create additional health risks.
- Family systems are affected by financial strain, influencing children and caregivers alike.
- Resources and organizations exist that can help reduce the financial burden and restore hope.
- Resilience practices from stress relief to community support ease the toll, even when financial stress cannot disappear overnight.
- Awareness empowers small steps that ease both financial and physical pressure.

CHAPTER 10

Lifestyle Integrations

Living with autoimmunity is about learning balance. There is no magic formula, no single diet, or one exercise routine that cures everything. But daily choices, such as food, movement, stress relief, and connection, can change how the body responds. Lifestyle integration means weaving these practices into everyday life in realistic, non-overwhelming ways.

Nutrition Basics

Food is information for the body. Anti-inflammatory choices, such as colorful vegetables, fruits, lean proteins, omega-rich fats, and whole grains, help calm overactive immune responses. Hydration is equally important, since dehydration can worsen fatigue, joint stiffness, and brain fog.

Balance is key. Strict elimination diets may help some people discover triggers, but living in constant restriction can increase stress and reduce quality of life. The goal is not perfection but awareness, noticing which foods fuel energy and which spark inflammation.

Movement

Exercise is often misunderstood in the context of autoimmune care. For some, overexertion causes flare-ups; for others, inactivity worsens pain and stiffness. The sweet spot is gentle, consistent movement: walking, stretching, yoga, tai chi, or light strength training.

During flares, rest may be necessary, but small movements, such as gentle stretching or deep breathing, help keep circulation flowing. Over time, movement builds strength, supports joint health, and improves mood. Consistency matters more than intensity.

Stress Management

Autoimmune flares are often stress-sensitive. Daily reset practices are crucial: short breathwork sessions, journaling emotions, mindfulness breaks, or guided meditations. These practices regulate cortisol, cool inflammation, and remind the body it is safe.

Reframing is another powerful tool. Instead of "I can't do this anymore," try "I'm listening to what my body needs today." Words shape chemistry. Stress management is not just about relaxation; it is about reclaiming power over how stress is processed.

Community & Connection

Healing is not a solo journey. Isolation increases anxiety and lowers resilience. Whether through a faith group, supportive family, therapy, or peer support, connection provides strength. Sharing stories reduces shame and builds hope.

Spiritual connection can also be an anchor, a prayer, meditation, or simply feeling part of something larger than yourself. These practices create perspective and peace in times of uncertainty.

Putting It into Practice

Lifestyle integration is not about doing everything at once. Start small:

- Add one anti-inflammatory meal a day.
- Commit to 10 minutes of movement.
- Set aside five minutes for breathing or journaling.
- Check in weekly with a trusted friend or support group.

Progress is progress. Each step forward is evidence of resilience.

Stories of Real People

Sofia, 33, living with rheumatoid arthritis, began by swapping soda for herbal tea and walking 15 minutes three times a week. Within months, her energy improved, and her flares became less intense.

James, 52, with multiple sclerosis, joined a men's support group. Talking openly about his struggles eased his depression, and he found new motivation to follow through with his physical therapy exercises.

Reflection & Worksheets

Reflection Questions:

- What small habit could I start this week to support my health?
- Which lifestyle areas (food, movement, stress, community) feel strongest right now? Which feels weakest?
- How does my body respond when I honor rest versus when I push too hard?
- Who can I lean on when stress feels overwhelming?

Lifestyle Integration Log (use as a simple daily/weekly journal):

- Area of focus: _____
- Today's choice: _____
- How it felt: _____
- What I'll try next: _____

Key Takeaways

- Lifestyle changes matter, but perfection is not required.
- Nutrition, movement, stress management, and community together create resilience.
- Small daily steps build habits that strengthen the body's ability to handle stress and inflammation.
- Integration is about progress, not a cure.

APPENDIX

TOOLS & RESOURCES

Autoimmunity isn't only about understanding; it's about **having tools**. Use these worksheets, logs, and guides to track patterns, plan flare days, prepare for appointments, and build daily resilience. (This content is educational and supportive, not medical advice. Always work with your care team.)

How to Use This Appendix

- Print the pages you'll use weekly.
- Keep one master binder and a small "daily kit" (journal + meds + water + snack).
- Revisit monthly to celebrate progress and adjust.

Symptom Tracker: Daily/Weekly

Daily Log:

- Date: _____
- Energy (0–10): _____
- Sleep quality/hours: _____
- Main symptoms (pain, stiffness, brain fog, digestion, mood): _____
- Possible triggers (food, stress, weather, activity): _____
- Meds/supplements taken (yes/no/notes): _____
- What helped today: _____
- Notes for tomorrow: _____

Weekly Reflection:

- Wins I noticed: _____
- Patterns or triggers I see: _____
- One adjustment I'll try next week: _____

Flare Map (Once per month)

- Earliest warning signs I notice: _____
- Typical length of a flare for me: _____
- What makes it worse: _____
- What reliably helps: _____
- People I can text/call: _____

Flare-Day Action Plan (Post on fridge)

Early Signs (what I feel first): _____

Immediate Steps (15–30 minutes):

- Hydrate: _____
- Breath reset (technique + minutes): _____
- Gentle movement/stretch: _____
- Nutrition (simple anti-inflammatory snack/meal): _____
- Medication protocol as prescribed: _____

Pacing Plan (today):

- Must-do tasks (keep tiny): _____
- Can shift/cancel: _____
- Rest windows (times): _____

Communication:

- Autoreply/text script: "I'm in a health day, I'll respond within ___."
- Who I'll update (name + time): _____

Aftercare (24–48 hrs):

- Warm bath/heat/ice: _____
- Light walk/mobility: _____
- Journal one page on what helped: _____

Emergency Notes (red flags from my doctor):

_____

Provider to call first: _____ Phone: _____

Medication & Labs Organizer

Current Medications/Supplements:

- Name / Dose / Time(s): _____
- Purpose: _____
- Side effects to watch: _____
- Refills due: _____ (set reminders)

Lab Tracker (write results + date):

- Thyroid: TSH, Free T4, T3, TPO/Tg antibodies: _____

- Inflammation: CRP, ESR: _____
- Autoimmune screens: ANA pattern/titer: _____

- Nutrients: Vitamin D, B12, Ferritin: _____

- Metabolic: A1C, CMP, Lipids: _____
- Disease-specific labs (list yours): _____

Questions to Ask at Next Visit:

- "Given my pattern, which labs matter most this quarter?"
- "How will we measure progress?"
- "What are my medication 'red flag' symptoms?"
- "Can we simplify my regimen to improve adherence?"

Doctor Visit Prep Kit

Before the Visit (10–15 minutes):

- Top three concerns: 1) ___ 2) ___ 3) ___
- One win since last visit: _____
- Symptom snapshots (bring 1–2 recent pages):
  _____
- Current meds list updated (yes/no):
  _____

During the Visit:

- Plain-language summary: "Here's what's getting in the way day-to-day."
- Ask: "What is the goal between now and the next visit?"
- Confirm: "What should trigger a call vs. urgent care?"

After the Visit:

- Next steps I understand: _____
- Labs/Imaging scheduled: _____

- Follow-up date: _____
- My one action this week: _____

Insurance/Appeal Script (save to phone):

- "I'm calling to confirm coverage for [test/med]. My diagnosis is [____]. If it's denied, please note I'm requesting the **specific reason** for denial and the **peer-to-peer** review option with my provider."

Nutrition Toolkit

Pantry Staples (budget-friendly):

- Whole grains (oats, brown rice, quinoa)
- Beans/lentils; canned fish (salmon, sardines, tuna)
- Olive/avocado oil; nuts/seeds
- Frozen fruits/vegetables; broth; spices (turmeric, ginger, garlic, cinnamon)

Gentle 7-Day Reset (outline):

- Mornings: protein + fiber (eggs/oats + berries)
- Midday: leafy salad or veggie-heavy bowl + protein
- Evenings: simple protein + two veggies + grain or potato
- Snacks: fruit + nuts; yogurt; hummus + veggies
- Hydration goal (your number): _____ per day

Trigger Exploration (optional, time-boxed):

- 2–4 weeks: remove **one** suspected trigger (e.g., ultra-processed foods or a specific category agreed with your clinician)
- Re-introduce slowly; note symptoms 24–72 hours

Meal Builder (write in):

- Protein: _____
- Veg 1: _____ Veg 2: _____
- Smart carb: _____
- Healthy fat/flavor: _____

Movement Toolkit

Daily 10-Minute Menu (choose 1–2):

- 5 min gentle neck/shoulder + 5 min hips/low back
- 10 min walk (or 2 × 5 min)
- 10 min yoga flow (child's pose, cat-cow, low lunge, forward fold)
- Bed-based mobility on flare days (ankle pumps, pelvic tilts, diaphragmatic breathing)

Weekly Rhythm (write your plan):

- Mon: _____
- Tue: _____
- Wed: _____
- Thu: _____
- Fri: _____
- Sat: _____
- Sun: _____

Pacing & Energy Envelope:

- My "Too Much" signs: _____
- Safe exertion window most days: _____
- Recovery go-to's: _____

Nervous System Toolkit

Breath Library (pick what fits today):

- Box breathing 4–4–4–4 (1–3 min)
- 4–7–8 wind-down (4 reps)
- Resonance breathing (~6 breaths/min for 5–10 min)
- Long exhale sighs (10–15 reps)

Grounding & Vagus Support:

- 5-senses check (name 5–4–3–2–1)
- Humming/gargling; gentle face/ear massage
- Cold water face splash (10–20 sec as tolerated)

Fast Micro-Resets (set phone cues):

- Top of the hour: 60-second breath check
- Lunch: 3-minute step outside
- Evening: 5-minute body scan

Thought Reframes (keep a list):

- "My body isn't failing; it's asking for care."
- "Progress beats perfection."
- "Rest is productive for healing."

Journaling Prompts:

- "What felt heavy today? What helped?"
- "A tiny win I can build on is…"
- "If my body could speak, it would say…"

Sleep Reset

Wind-Down Builder (30–60 minutes):

- Screens off by: _____
- Lights lowered / warm lamp on (yes/no)
- Ritual (bath, stretch, read, prayer): _____
- Caffeine cut-off time: _____
- Morning light exposure plan: _____

If You Wake at Night:

- No problem-solving; brief breath set
- Note worry on paper - "park it"
- Gentle body scan - back to sleep or restful quiet

Family & Caregiver Guide

How to Help Me During a Flare (card):

- Best contact method: _____
- What helps most: _____
- What to avoid: _____
- If urgent, please: _____

Boundaries That Protect My Health:

- "I can visit for ___ minutes, then I need to rest."
- "I appreciate advice, but today I just need listening."
- "I'll confirm morning-of based on symptoms."

Caregiver Check-In (for them):

- "What support do **you** need this week?"
- "Where can we ask for extra help?"

Financial Relief & Advocacy (Quick Access)

Steps That Help:

- Gather documents: diagnoses, meds list, last 2–3 EOBs, denials
- Call insurer: ask coverage, appeal paths, case manager option
- Ask providers for **payment plans** and **cash-pay discounts**
- Apply to **patient assistance programs** for meds/tests

Organizations to Explore (examples):

- Patient Advocate Foundation (case management, financial navigation)
- NeedyMeds (drug assistance lookups)
- Disease-specific groups (e.g., Lupus Foundation of America, National MS Society)
- Local 211 / community resource lines (food, utilities, transport)

- Hospital social work departments (grants, charity care)

Payment Plan Script (use or adapt):

- "I'm committed to paying this bill. I'm requesting a no-interest payment plan of $___/month and any available discounts or charity programs. Who can authorize that today?"

Pregnancy & Early Development Toolkit

Preconception Checklist:

- Optimize sleep, nutrition, movement
- Reduce alcohol/smoking, review meds with clinician
- Manage stress; begin prenatal with folate per provider
- Discuss family history and lab screening

During Pregnancy (awareness without blame):

- Gentle nutrition + hydration; simplify products at home
- Stress support: breath, prayer, safe connection
- Ask providers about meds, imaging, and exposures
- If using a surrogate: ensure support for her health and stress needs

Questions for Care Team:

- "Which exposures should I avoid or limit?"

- "What's our plan if I flare during pregnancy?"
- "How will we monitor the baby's growth and my immune status?"

Blood Type & Health: Quick Reference

- Type O - robust immune responses; watch digestive stress; prioritize gut soothing and steady meals.
- Type A - stress-sensitive; support thyroid/adrenals; emphasize mind-body resets and gentle movement.
- Type B - balanced tendencies; maintain consistency, hydration, and infection prevention.
- Type AB - mixed traits; prioritize stress reduction, circulation support, grounding routines.

📌 Patterns, not predictions. Personalize with your clinician.

Safety & Red Flags

Call your provider or urgent care if you notice:

- New severe chest pain, shortness of breath, or one-sided weakness
- High fever not responding to meds or signs of infection while immunosuppressed
- Sudden vision changes, severe new headache, or confusion
- Any medication reaction your doctor flagged as urgent

Emergency Info Card (carry in wallet):

- Name / DOB: _____
- Diagnoses: _____
- Medications/allergies: _____
- Emergency contact: _____
- Treating physician/clinic: _____ Phone: _____

Reproducible Forms Index (for easy printing)

- Daily/Weekly Symptom Log
- Flare-Day Action Plan
- Medication & Labs Organizer
- Doctor Visit Prep Kit
- Nutrition: 7-Day Reset + Meal Builder
- Movement: 10-Minute Menu + Weekly Rhythm
- Nervous System Toolkit (Breath + Grounding)
- Sleep Wind-Down Builder
- Family & Caregiver Cards
- Financial Relief Scripts & Notes
- Pregnancy & Early Development Toolkit
- Emergency Info Card

Final Encouragement

Healing is not linear. Use these pages as companions, not scorecards. Every small step is a signal of safety to your body and a seed of resilience for tomorrow.

Thank you for your purchase. You can also follow us online on IG and FanBase @SpeakingFreedom, You can find our YouTube Channel yourtube.com/@speakingfreedomTV

Please check out our other books.

Faith 101

Faith 201

Faith 301

Faith 401

The Unknown Power

Spiritual Human

Behavior It's My Time

Oops I Joined a Cult

No Religion, Just God

Messengers Among Us

Beyond The Veil

Understanding Immunity

www.ingramcontent.com/pod-product-compliance
Lightning Source LLC
Chambersburg PA
CBHW070145080526
44586CB00015B/1847